BUSINESS
Reward

INSHAMAMUL HAQ

Copy right @puplic domain
& author

ISBN:9781312070370

DEDICATION

I am grateful to dedicate this book to my family members for their unconditional support

ACKNOWLEDGMENT

I acknowledge to god for showing grace on me to educate.

I also acknowledge each and every person who give support and motivated for paper back.

CONTENTS

SYNONYMOUS OF BUSINESS	6
FUNDAMENTAL OF BUSINESS	9
THEORIES OF BUSINESS	14
BUSINESS MODELS	28
PILLARS OF BUSINESS	42
METHODS OF BUSINESS	54
BUSINESS EVOLUTION	65

BOTTOM LINE	71

SYNONYMOUS OF BUSINESS

The word business comes from the word busy, and means doing things. It works on regular basis

Business refers to an organization or enterprising entity engaged in commercial, industrial, or professional activities. The purpose of a business is to organize some sort of economic production of goods or services

Some businesses run as small operations in a single industry while others are large operations that spread across many industries around the world.

Business can earn a profit for the products and services it offers.

.They can be commercial, industrial, or others. For-profit business entities do business to earn a profit, while non-profit ones do it for a charitable mission. Business ownership includes partnerships, sole proprietorships, corporations, etc. Businesses can be small-or large scale

EXAMPLES:

    Walmart & apple

Peter Drucker was a business consultant, lecturer, and author. He is known as the "Father of Modern Management" because of his numerous works and seminars on management theory and practice

One needs to take various steps before starting a business. One must conduct market research first and then develop a business plan. The next step must be to seek capital or other funding and select a location and business structure. It is also important to pick the right name, complete the registration process, and get the tax documents and essential permits. A bank account is a must before starting a business.

An online business is different from a traditional business. You need to design your website after your market research, business plan development, and paperwork formalities. After that, start finding ways to build up your target market and engage your audience with social media

FUNDAMENTAL OF BUSINESS

Many of the fundamental which needed for the business.

- Marketing and branding.
- Financial management.
- Accounting
- Strategic management.
- Research and development.

- People management.
- Legal considerations.
- Vendor management.

For businesses, such as profitability, revenue, assets, liabilities, and growth potential are considered fundamentals

Through the use of fundamental analysis, you may calculate a company's financial ratios to determine the feasibility of the investment.

Fundamentals provide a method to set the financial value of a company, security, or currency.Included in fundamental analysis is basic qualitative and quantitative information that contributes to the asset's financial or economic well-being.

Macroeconomic fundamentals include topics that affect an economy at large. Microeconomic fundamentals focus on the activities within smaller segments of the economy.

In business and economics, fundamentals represent the primary characteristics and financial data necessary to determine the stability and health of an asset. This data can include macroeconomic, or large-scale factors, and microeconomic, or small-scale factors to set a value on securities or businesses.

Analysts and investors examine these fundamentals to develop an estimate as to whether the underlying asset is considered a worthwhile investment, and if there is fair valuation in the market.

For businesses, information such as profitability, revenue, assets, liabilities, and growth potential are considered fundamentals with the use of 0 analysis, you may calculate a company's financial ratios to determine the feasibility of the investment.

Business cycle

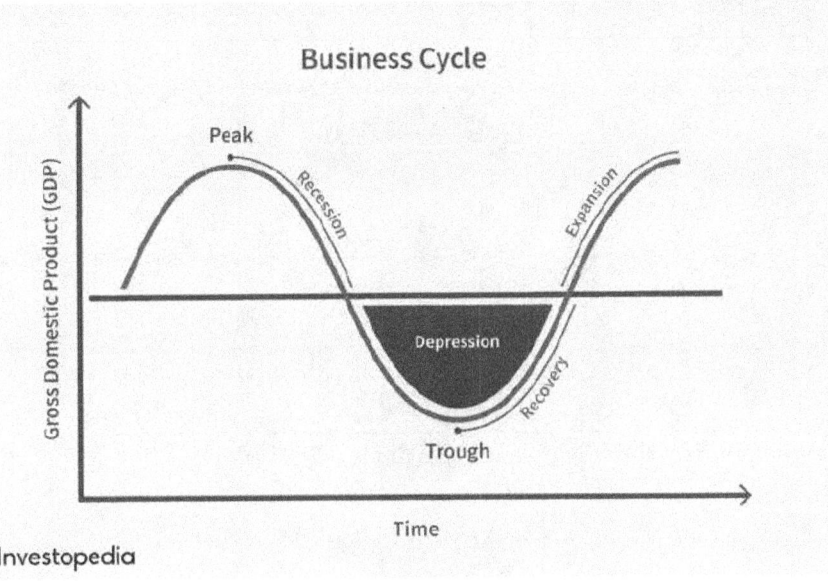

Business cycles are a type of fluctuation found in the aggregate economic activity of a nation -- a cycle that consists of expansions occurring at about the same time in many economic activities, followed by similarly general contractions (recessions). This sequence of changes is recurrent but

What is a Recession?

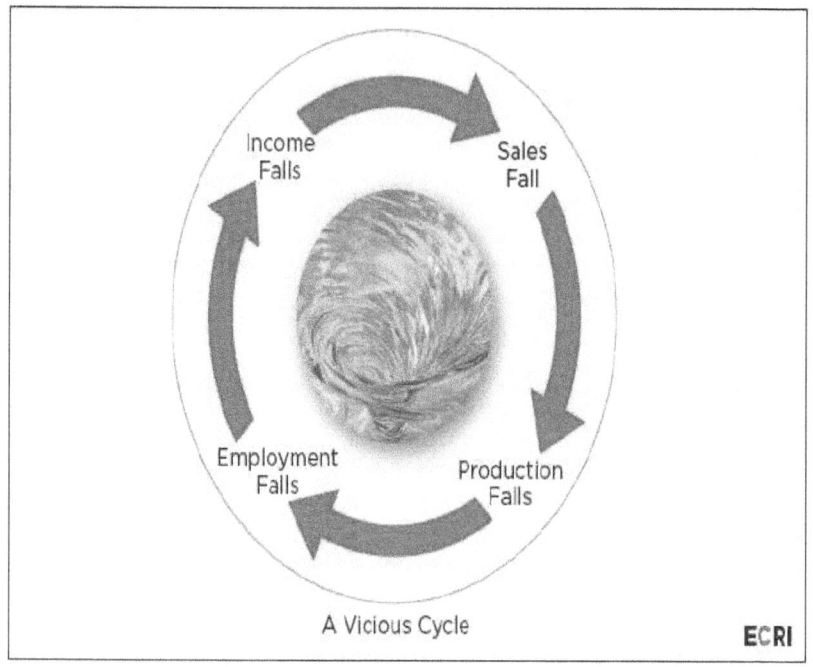

A Vicious Cycle

not periodic.

The business cycle is an example of an economic cycle.

A recession is the part of an economic cycle that involves an economic contraction. One popular definition of recession is two consecutive quarters of economic contraction.

THEORIES OF BUSINESS

These theories can be grouped into five main categories: classical management theories, behavioral management theories, systems theory, contingency theory, and Modern Management Theories.

Each theory has its own unique perspective on how to best manage an organization.

In theory and practice, the term business model is used for a broad range of informal and formal descriptions to represent core aspects of an organization or business, including purpose, business process, target customers, offerings, strategies, infrastructure, organizational structures, sourcing, trading practices.

Understanding organizations comes from understanding management theory, and Kimani outlines four major management theories for the basis of organizations: bureaucratic theory, scientific management theory, behavioural management theory, and human relations theory.

Peter Drucker believed that a successful manager needs to understand subjects like psychology, science, and be guided by ethical and moral principles.

He encouraged creative rather than bureaucratic management and insisted that managers should, above all else, be leaders.

A number of theories have been developed by different economists from time to time to understand the concept of business cycles. In the first half of twentieth century, various new and important concepts related to business cycles come into existence.

Some of the most important theories of business cycles are

Pure Monetary Theory:

The traditional business cycle theorists take into consideration the monetary and credit system of an economy to analyze business cycles. Therefore, theories developed by these traditional theorists are called monetary theory of business cycle.

The monetary theory states that the business cycle is a result of changes in monetary and credit market conditions.

Hartery, the main supporter of this theory, advocated that business cycles are the continuous phases of inflation and deflation. According to him, changes in an economy take place due to changes in the flow of money.

For example, when there is increase in money supply, there would be increase in prices, profits, and total output. This results in the growth of an economy. On the other hand, a fall in money supply would result in decrease in prices, profit, and total output, which would lead to decline of an economy. Apart from this, Hartery also advocated that the main factor that influences the flow of money is credit mechanism. In economy, the banking system plays an important role in increasing money flow by providing credit.

An economy shows growth when the volume of bank credit increases. This increase in the growth continues till the volume of bank credit increases. Banks offer credit facilities to individuals or organizations due to the fact that banks find it profitable to provide credit on easy terms.

The easy availability of funds from banks helps organizations to perform various business activities. This leads to increase in various investment opportunities, which further results in deepening and widening of capital.

Apart from this, credit provided by banks on easy terms helps organizations to expand their production.

An economy shows growth when the volume of bank credit increases. This increase in the growth continues till the volume of bank credit increases. Banks offer credit facilities to individuals or organizations due to the fact that banks find it profitable to provide credit on easy terms.

Monetary Over-Investment Theory:

Monetary over-investment theory focuses mainly on the imbalance between actual and desired investments. According to this theory, the actual investment is much higher than the desired investment. This theory was given by Hayek.

According to him, the investment and consumption patterns of an economy should match with each other to bring the economy in equilibrium.

For stabilizing this equilibrium, the voluntary savings should be equal to actual investment in an economy.

In an economy, generally, the total investment is distributed among industries in such a way that each industry produces products to a limit, so that its demand and supply are equal. This implies that the investment at every level and for every product in the whole economy is equal. As a result, there would be no expansion and contraction and the economy would always be in equilibrium.

According to this theory, changes in economic conditions would occur only when the money supply and investment-saving relations show fluctuations. The investment-saving relations are affected when there is an increase in investment opportunities and voluntary savings are constant.

Investment opportunities increase due to several reasons, such as low interest rates, increased marginal efficiency of capital, and increase in expectations of businessmen.

Apart from this, when banks start supporting industries for investment by lending money at lower rates, it results in an increase in investment.

This may result in the condition of overinvestment mainly in capital good industries. In such a case, investment and savings increase, but the consumption remains unaffected as there is no change in consumer goods

Consequently, profit increases with increase in investment opportunities, which further results in an increase in the demand for various products and services.

The demand for products and services exceeds the supply of products and services.

This leads to inflation in the economy, which reduces the purchasing power of individuals. Therefore, with decrease in the purchasing power of individuals, the real demand for products does not increase at the same rate at which the investment increases. The real investment is done at the cost of real consumption.

The balance between the investment and consumer demand is disturbed. As a result, it is difficult to maintain the current rate of investment. The demand of consumer goods would be dependent on the income of individuals.

Schumpeter's Theory of Innovation:

The other theories of business cycles lay emphasis on investment and monetary expansion. The Schumpeter's theory of innovation advocates that business innovations are responsible for rapid changes in investment and business fluctuations.

According to Schumpeter said, "Business cycles are almost exclusively the result of innovations in the industrial and commercial organization.

Innovations are such changes of the combination of the factors of production as cannot be effected by infinitesimal steps or variations on the margin.

Innovation consists primarily in changes in methods of production and transportation, or changes in industrial organization, or in the production of a new article, or opening of a new market or of new sources of material."

He also said, innovation refers to an application of a new technique of production or new machinery or a new concept to reduce cost and increase profit.

In addition, he propounded that innovations are responsible for the occurrence of business cycles. He also designed a model having two stages, namely, first approximation and second approximation.

KEYNES THEORY

Keynes theory was developed in 1930s,

which was the period when whole world was going through great depression. This theory is the reply of

Keynes to classical economists.

According to classical economists, if there is high unemployment condition in an economy, then economic forces, such as demand and supply, would act in a manner to bring back full employment condition.

Keynes has proposed three types of propensities to understand business cycles. These are propensity to save, propensity to consume, and propensity of marginal efficiency of capital.

He has also developed a concept of multiplier that represents changes in income level produced by the changes in investment.

He also advocated that the expansion of business cycle occurs due to increase in marginal efficiency of capital. This encourages investors to invest

Samuelson's Model of Multiplier Accelerator Interaction:

The economists of post-Keynesian period emphasized the need of both multiplier and accelerator concepts to explain business cycles.

Samuelson's model of multiplier accelerator interaction was the first model that represents interaction between these two concepts.

In his model, Samuelson has described the way the multiplier and accelerator interact with each other for generating income and increasing consumption and demand of investment. He also describes how these two factors are responsible for creating economic fluctuations.

Samuelson used two concepts, namely, autonomous and derived investment, to explain his model.

Autonomous investment refers to the investment due to exogenous factors, such as new product and production.

Samuelson made certain assumptions for the explanation of business cycles. Some of the assumptions are that the production capacity is limited and consumption takes place after a gap of one year.

Another assumption made by him is that there would be a gap of one year between the increase in consumption and increase in the demand of investment. In addition, he assumed that there would be no government activity and foreign trade in the economy. According to the assumption given by Samuelson that there would be no government activity and foreign trade, the equilibrium would be achieved when

$Y_t = C_t + I_t$

Where, Y_t = National income

C_t = Total consumption expenditure

I_t = Investment expenditure t = Time period

Hicks's Theory:

Hicks has associated business cycles to the growth theory of Harrod-Domar. According to him, business cycles take place simultaneously with economic growth; therefore, business cycles should be explained in association with the growth theory.

In his theory, he has used the following concepts to explain business cycles:

a. Saving-investment relation and multiplier concepts given by Keynes

b. Acceleration concept given by Clark

c. Multiplier-acceleration interaction concepts given by Samuelson

d. Growth model of Harrod-Domar

Hicks has also framed certain assumptions for describing business cycle concept.

Most common theory mainly used to function both large and small scale business are normally known as **organization** theory.

organizational theories

Social and behavioral scientists have developed various theories to describe the correct way to understand and approach the key to an organization's productivity and success. These organizational theories discuss different ways that managers and supervisors may address their leadership responsibilities in order to yield the most productive and efficient results.

Organization theory classified into six primary

1. CLASSICAL THEORY

> *Classical theory can address the primary aspects of a business's formal organizational structure. This theory discusses how to divide up professional tasks in the most efficient and effective way.*

Classical theorists pay particular attention to the professional dynamics and relationships within an organization and how these relationships may impact the company's function and production.

The underlying purpose of this theory is to help businesses create the most beneficial structures within a company that can then help the organization accomplish its goals.

The four principles of the classical theory include:

Division of labor: This principle argues that the production of a commodity splits into various divisions of manufacturing, and the people work within each division according to their area of specialization. This process results in maximum product output with minimum expenses.

Scalar and functional processes: The scalar process deals with a company's vertical growth, meaning the relationships between business leaders and their employees. This means that professionals in management instruct their employees, and employees carry out the actions.

Structure: The principle of structure

describes patterns of professional behavior that lead to the accomplishment of the organization's goals. Structure is a tool that may facilitate relationships between all aspects of the company or business.

Span of control: The span of control means attributing the appropriate numbers of employees to a supervisor so they can implement the principles of coordination, planning, motivation and leadership. This is about assigning the maximum number of employees to a manager while also allowing them enough time and support to lead their staff.

2. Neo-classical theory

Beginning with the Hawthorne studies in the 1920s, the neo-classical theory focuses on the emotional and psychological components of peoples' behavior in an organization. Sociologists and psychologists found topics like leadership, morale and cooperation contribute to professional habits and behaviors.

This theory argues that a sense of belonging and social acceptance is an important aspect of positive performance in the workplace. This means that effective leaders understand how the group dynamics may contribute to the success of the organization overall.

Business leaders may implement systems and strategies to improve the of their employees and facilitate meaningful professional connections through motivation, counseling and communication.

3. **Modern theory**

Modern theory, also called modern organizational theory, includes multiple management development approaches. This theory considers interactions between people within an organization and the surrounding environment, as well as the interpersonal interactions between members of the organization.

Theorists based this approach on systems analysis and used both quantitative and behavioral sciences to develop it.

That professional leaders who adopt this theory may use statistical and mathematical information to make business decisions.

Those who implement this theoretical approach may require an skills in-depth and knowledge of their employees'.

Behaviors in order to implement programs that further their productivity and professional development.

4. **Contingency theory**

Contingency theory, also called decision theory, views organizations as a structure composed of choice-makers, and argues that there is no one right way to make a decision.

Herbert A. Simon, a primary contributor to this theory, found that while people make business decisions at all levels of an organization, employees working at higher levels make the most valuable or impactful choices.

Theory argues that the ideal decision or choice may differ from one to another, so choices are   internal and external factors. means that the success of a business is contingent on the decisions made by the organization's leaders.

Some believe that management is responsible for analyzing business situations and then acting to address any issues or challenges.

5. **Motivation theory**

The motivational theory includes the study of what drives and inspires members of an organization to work toward their professional goals who support this approach argue that employees perform their job duties accurately and productively when management knows how to motivate them correctly.

This may require business leaders to thoroughly understand their workers' behavioral patterns and preferences to recognize the most beneficial way to support them.

The goal of this is to increase company productivity on the basis that appropriately encourages employees to perform more efficiently, thus increasing production and profit.

Coordinator may consider intrinsic and extrinsic factors that can impact their employees' feelings and experiences in order to develop effective systems and managerial strategies.

6. **Open systems theory**

Open systems theory is a concept that argues that an organization's environment influences it, and understanding the impact of this influence may help managers develop more effective leadership strategies.

Specific factors may include the

vendors or distributors that a company works with, industry competitors or government agencies that control or interact with production regulation.

Alternatively, general factors include four primary aspects that occur because of the geographic location of the organization.

These aspects include:

Economic conditions: The geographic location of a business can have a great impact on the company's ability to grow and remain successful because of local economic trends and events, including recessions and economic upswings.

Cultural values: The cultural values of a community can influence customers' viewpoints and standards. This may influence whether they support your business or organization, and business leaders may use this theory to adapt to local cultural ethics.

Education systems: Areas with strong education systems may be ideal for businesses that are in the technology industry or other companies that may rely on employees with extensive academic training.

Legal consideration: The legal and political environment, including the taxes and regulations on business operations, may impact the stability and security of an organization. This may influence its ability to remain productive and successful.

BUSINESS MODELS

The term business model refers to a company's plan for making a profit. It identifies the products or services the business plans to sell, its identified target market, and any anticipated expenses. Business models are important for both new and established businesses. They help new, developing companies attract investment, recruit talent, and motivate management and staff.

Business model is a high-level plan for profitably operating a business in a specific marketplace. A primary component of the business model is the value proposition.

This is a description of the goods or services that a company offers and why they are desirable to customers or clients, ideally stated in a way that differentiates the product or service from its competitors.

A new enterprise's business model should also cover projected startup costs and financing sources, the target customer base for the business, marketing strategy, a review of the competition, and projections of revenues and expenses. plan may also define opportunities in which the business can partner with other established companies. , the business model for an advertising business may identify benefits from arrangement for referrals to from a printing company

Types of Business Models

There are as many types of business models as there are types of business. For instance, direct sales, franchising, advertising-based, and brick-and-mortar stores are all examples of traditional business models. There are hybrid models as well, such as businesses that combine internet retail with brick-and-mortar stores or with sporting organizations like the NBA.

Retailer

One of the more common business models most people interact with regularly is the retailer model. A retailer is the last entity along a supply chain. They often buy finished goods from manufacturers or distributors and interface directly with customers.

Example: Costco Wholesale

Manufacturer

A manufacturer is responsible for sourcing raw materials and producing finished products by leveraging internal labor, machinery, and equipment. A manufacturer may make custom goods or highly replicated, mass produced products. A manufacturer can also sell goods to distributors, retailers, or directly to customers.

Example: Ford Motor Company

Fee-for-Service

Instead of selling products, fee-for-service business models are centered around labor and providing services.

A fee-for-service business model may charge by an hourly rate or a fixed cost for a specific agreement.

Fee-for-service companies are often specialized, offering insight that may not be common knowledge or may require specific training.

Example: DLA Piper LLP

Subscription

Subscription-based business models strive to attract clients in the hopes of luring them into long-time, loyal patrons. This is done by offering a product that requires ongoing payment, usually in return for a fixed duration of benefit. Though largely offered by digital companies for access to software, subscription business models are also popular for physical goods such as monthly reoccurring agriculture/produce subscription box deliveries.

Example: Spotify

Freemium

Freemium business models attract customers by introducing them to basic, limited-scope products. Then, with the client using their service, the company attempts to convert them to a more premium, advance product that requires payment. Although a customer may theoretically stay on freemium forever, a company tries to show the benefit of what becoming an upgraded member can hold.

Example: LinkedIn/LinkedIn Premium

Bundling

If a company is concerned about the cost of attracting a single customer, it may attempt to bundle products to sell multiple goods to a single client. Bundling capitalizes on existing customers by attempting to sell them different products. This can be incentivized by offering pricing discounts for buying multiple products.

Example: AT&T

Marketplace

Marketplaces are somewhat straight-forward: in exchange for hosting a platform for business to be conducted, the marketplace receives compensation.

Although transactions could occur without a marketplace, this business models attempts to make transacting easier, safer, and faster.

Example: eBay

Affiliate

Affiliate business models are based on marketing and the broad reach of a specific entity or person's platform.

Companies pay an entity to promote a good, and that entity often receives compensation in exchange for their promotion. That compensation may be a fixed payment, a percentage of sales derived from their promotion, or both.

Example: social media influencers such as Lele Pons, Zach King, or Chiara Ferragni.

Razor Blade

Aptly named after the product that invented the model, this business model aims to sell a durable product below cost to then generate high-margin sales of a disposable component of that product.

Also referred to as the "razor and blade model", razor blade companies may give away expensive blade handles with the premise that consumers need to continually buy razor blades in the long run.

Example: HP (printers and ink)

Reverse Razor Blade

Instead of relying on high-margin companion products, a reverse razor blade business model tries to sell a high-margin product upfront. Then, to use the product, low or free companion products are provided. This model aims to promote that upfront sale, as further use of the product is not highly profitable.

Example: Apple (iPhones + applications)

Franchise

The franchise business model leverages existing business plans to expand and reproduce a company at a different location. Often food, hardware, or fitness companies, franchisers work with incoming franchisees to finance the business, promote the new location, and oversee operations. In return, the franchisor receives a percentage of earnings from the franchisee.

Example: Domino's Pizza

Pay-As-You-Go

Instead of charging a fixed fee, some companies may implement a pay-as-you-go business model where the amount charged depends on how much of the product or service was used.

The company may charge a fixed fee for offering the service in addition to an amount that changes each month based on what was consumed.

Example: Utility companies

Brokerage

A brokerage business model connects buyers and sellers without directly selling a good themselves.

Brokerage companies often receive a percentage of the amount paid when a deal is finalized.

Most common in real estate, brokers are also prominent in construction/development or freight.

Example: ReMax

Business Model Examples for Social Enterprises

- The Entrepreneur Support

Model. ...

- The Market Intermediary Model. ...
- The Employment Model. ...
- The Fee-for-Service Model. ...
- The Low-income Client Model. ...
- The Cooperative Model. ...
- The Market Linkage Model. ...
- The Service Subsidization Model.

PILLARS OF BUSINESS

Every business needs a handle

on the four pillars of business:

management,

marketing,

operations and

finance.

If you are feeling overwhelmed, let's take it step-by-step. Entering into entrepreneurship can be frightening, but you will be okay if you follow a roadmap for success

Don't become so overwhelmed with everything you need to do that you get stuck in analysis paralysis. Entrepreneurship is hard, but it's not impossible.

Businessman and author Peter Drucker once said, "Whenever you see a successful business, someone once made a courageous decision." What's required of you is to keep learning and practice what you have learned. There is no timeline to follow but your own.

To create and run a successful business, you need to know the needs of your customer and serve them better than others in your market. Here's what you need to consider for each pillar:

Management. How will you handle the process of serving your customer? How are customers getting in contact with you? What services/products are they purchasing? How can you ensure that they are receiving everything they are expecting? You need to manage the customer journey of your business.

Marketing. How will new customers find you? What digital marketing assets are you using to establish your brand? What local community collaborations are you making to spread news of your business? You need to market your business to find new customers and keep your sales pipeline full.

Operations. How will you deliver the services/products to your customers? If you have a team, how will you all work together as a team to deliver services/products? What tools, technologies and systems do you need in place to run a successful operation?

Finance. Business's account for your business and keep these finances separate from your personal accounts. Trust me, the sooner you get organized here the better prepared you will be when tax season comes around

Business has three main components;

1. Sales & Marketing

2. Operations & Fulfilments

3. Finance & Accounting

business as being situated on a three-legged pedestal. If one of the legs fail, your business is prone to stumble

Sales & Marketing

lf you fail to bring in fresh leads and you don't obtain new customers, there is no business!

Operations & Fulfilment

Operations include hiring the right people, purchasing the right equipment, making sure your software works as needed, etc.

Suppose your operations are in shambles and you don't deliver on your promises in a timely, qualitative, and satisfactory manner. In that case, your customer won't work with you again or buy your products. Even worse, they will refuse to pay you for the work they feel wasn't delivered as promised.

Finance & Accounting this will ensure that you set the right price and are profitable on every sale and job. Finance should ensure that you have the cash to hire and expand, as well as you have a written plan for growth. This is the part of your business that handles your books and records. Finance and accounting is the department that helps you with taxes and other legal compliance issues with the IRS and related agencies

METHODS OF BUSINESS

business methodology increases chances of success, prevents waste of time and effort, eliminates unnecessary actions, and ensures consistent reporting and analysis.

Types of business Methods

Standard Methods.

Procurement Methods.

Labour-Based Methods.

Intrascholastic Activities.

Products and Services.

Cannabis wholesaler.

Basic health plan services.

Supply Business.

Standard Methods means the examination and analytical procedures set forth in the most recent edition of "Standard Methods for the Examination of Water and Wastewater" published jointly by the American Public Health Association, the American Water Works Association, and the Water Pollution Control Federation.

Procurement Methods means any one of the procurement modes / methods as provided in the Punjab Procurement Rules 2014 published by the Punjab Procurement Regulatory

Authority (PPRA), Government of Punjab.

Labour-Based Methods means work methods whereby activities are carried out using Labour where technically and economically viable and appropriate equipment is only used when Labour alone will not achieve the required standards.

Intrascholastic Activities means athletic or non-athletic/academic activities where students compete with students from within the same school.

Products and Services means the products and/or services to be sold by Vendor hereunder as identified and described on Attachment A hereto and incorporated herein, as may be updated from time to time by Vendor to reflect products and/or services offered by Vendor generally to its customers.

Cannabis wholesaler means any licensed person or entity that purchases or otherwise obtains, stores, sells or otherwise transfers, and may transport, cannabis items for the purpose of resale or other transfer to either another cannabis wholesaler or to a cannabis retailer, but not to consumers.

Basic health plan services means that schedule of covered

Supply Business means the licensed business of the Licensee and any affiliate or related undertaking of the Licensee as a Supplier but shall not include the business carried out by the Board in its capacity as public electricity supplier;

Licensed Method means any method that is covered by Patent Rights the use of which would constitute, but for the license granted to LICENSEE under this Agreement, an infringement of any pending or issued and unexpired claim within Patent Rights.

Interscholastic Activities means athletic or non-athletic/academic activities where students compete on a school vs. school basis.

Specialized services means any

program or service designed and operated to serve primarily individuals with developmental disabilities, including a program or service provided by an entity licensed or certified by the department.

If there is a question as to whether a provider or entity under contract with a provider is providing specialized services, the provider or contract entity may request that the director of the department make a determination. The director's determination is final.

Goods and Services or "goods or services" means any work, labor, commodities, equipment, materials, or supplies of any tangible or intangible nature, except real property or any interest therein, provided or performed

BUSINESS EVOLUTION

Business history is a historiographical field which examines the history of firms, business methods, government regulation and the effects of business on society.

It also includes biographies of

individual firms, executives, and entrepreneurs. It is related to economic history.

The ancient age of business extended form the beginning of human civilization to the barter system. With the start of economic activities, resource-surplus and resource-deficit individuals were general features of the society.

As a result, man started exchange of commodities that was known as Barter System.

Beginning of business may be traced with the dawn of human civilization in the form of Barter System. Unlimited wants and limited resources and human efforts to balance these two are the basic feature of human life.

Economic activities are foundations of human life, existence and civilization.

The history of business evolution may be divided into three periods.

1. ANCIENT AGE
2. MIDDLE AGE
3. MODERN AGE

ANCIENT AGE

The ancient age of business extended form the beginning of human civilization to the barter system.

The start of economic activities, resource-surplus and resource-deficit individuals were general features of the society. As a result, man started exchange of commodities that was known as Barter System.

Gradually, different things were used as medium of exchange, which culminated into the invention of money, potters, blacksmiths, weavers, cultivators, etc., were the usual producers and businessmen of that day.

MIDDLE AGE

Middle age of business extended from the barter system up to

Industrial Revolution (IR) in the 18th century.

Invention of money or currency I e mental money, caused a revolution in the exchange. Business from developed and extended to partnership from proprietorship. Regional competition was a general phenomenon among the businessmen. Small-scale factory, production and use of technology were general characteristics of the production process.

To reduce competition and to enhance cooperation, different guild systems, such as merchant guild, craft guild, etc., evolved in the business arena. Monopoly and producer's oriented markets were dominant at that time.

MODERN AGE

MODERN AGE business started from the Industrial Revolution in the mid 1900s. Major scientific innovations transformed manual production process into mechanical one. Large-scale production, factory based industrial installation, expanded business operation were some of the characteristics of the business and production process after Industrial Revolution.

Some of the objectives of colonial expansion of the European colonial powers over Asia.

Africa and American countries were to create market for large-scale production and to collect raw materials for the industry. The conflict of colonial powers caused the ground for the happening of two World Wars. All these contributed to the gradual globalization of business operation.

BOTTOM LINE

The role of a business is to produce and distribute goods and services to satisfy a public need or demand.

According to Business News Daily corporate social responsibility (CSR) is "a business practice that involves participating in initiatives that benefit a society."

The Triple Bottom Line Defined." The BUSINESS is an accounting framework that incorporates three dimensions of performance: **social, environmental and financial**.

PREFERENCES :

LINK. IN

AUTHOR: ANTHONY FLYNN

PUBLISHED ON 21 Jan 2020

https://www.investopedia.com/

AUTHOR: CHRISTINA MAJASKI

PUBLISHED ON 29 May 2021

www.ingramcontent.com/pod-product-compliance
Lightning Source LLC
Chambersburg PA
CBHW070427180526
45158CB00017B/912